Gallery Books
Editor: Peter Fallon

TRANSLATIONS

Michael Hartnett

TRANSLATIONS

Edited by Peter Fallon

Gallery Books

Translations
is first published
simultaneously in paperback
and in a clothbound edition
on 11 September 2003.

The Gallery Press
Loughcrew
Oldcastle
County Meath
Ireland

ISBN 1 85235 323 6 (*paperback*)
     1 85235 324 4 (*clothbound*)

A CIP catalogue record for this book
is available from the British Library.

The Gallery Press acknowledges the financial assistance
of An Chomhairle Ealaíon / The Arts Council, Ireland.

Contents

Tao *page* 11
Sikong Tu Walks in the Forest 29
Catullus 36
The Hag of Beare 52
Marbán, a Hermit, Speaks 56
'Calling bell . . .' 59
'He is my love . . .' 60
'Eve, I, wife to the first man . . .' 61
'Have mercy on me, O Trinity . . .' 62
'Ach! this new Irish fashion and ach! . . .' 64
'On getting up one morning . . .' 65
Last Lines 67
Lament for Tadhg Cronin's Children 68
Carraig na bhFear 69
O'Sullivan's Malediction 72
The Connerys 74
Heine 76
Gypsy Ballads
    BALLAD OF THE MOON 84
    PRECIOSA AND THE WIND 86
    THE FIGHT 88
    THE SLEEPWALKING BALLAD 90
    THE GYPSY NUN 93
    THE UNFAITHFUL WIFE 94
    BALLAD OF THE BLACK SORROW 96
    SAN MIGUEL 98
    SAN RAFAEL 100
    GABRIEL 102
    THE ARREST OF ANTONIO EL CAMBORIO
       ON THE ROAD TO SEVILLE 104
    THE DEATH OF ANTONIO EL CAMBORIO 106
    DEAD FROM LOVE 108
    BALLAD OF THE ACCURSÈD 110
    BALLAD OF THE SPANISH CIVIL GUARD 112

In Memoriam David Hayes, Latin Teacher 116
Delver 118
Celebration 119
This Lonely Load 121
Oriental Morning 122
Portrait 124

An Afterword: Peter Fallon 126

Original Languages

Chinese 11, 29
German 76-82
Irish (Old) 52, 56, 59
  (Middle) 60, 61
  (Modern) 62, 64, 65, 67, 68, 69, 72,
    74, 119, 121, 122, 124
Latin 36-48, 116
Latvian 118
Spanish 84-112

Authors

Anonymous (Old Irish) 52, 56, 59
  (Middle Irish) 60, 61
  (Modern Irish) 65, 74
Catullus, Gaius Valerius 36-48
Hartnett, Michael (Ó hAirtnéide, Mícheál) 124
Heine, Heinrich 76-82
Horace (Quintus Horatius Flaccus) 116
? Lao-tzu 11
Lorca, Federico García 84-112
Mac Con Midhe, Giolla Brighde 62
? Mac Giolla Phádraig, Brian 64
Ní Dhomhnaill, Nuala 119-122
Ó Bruadair, Dáibhí 67
Ó Murchú na Ráithíneach, Seán 69
Ó Rathaille, Aodhagán 68
Ó Súilleabháin, Eoghan Rua 72
Sikong Tu 29
Ziedonis, Imants 118

A note on Tao

This is not a translation. I know no Chinese. In 1963 I was curator of Joyce's Tower in Sandycove. I read a Victorian translation of the *Tao Te Ching* and could see the beauty of the poetry and of the philosophy beneath the translator's ugly prose. I did this version to satisfy myself. The imagery is a mixture of Oriental, Occidental and mystical. The landscape is that of Sandycove, the tower and the sea. I hope that after all this tampering the philosophy at least is intact.

Tao

based on the Chinese Tao Te Ching,
attributed to Lao-tzu, ?born c.570 BC

1   It is not to be worded,
the path of the knowing person.
All that I know and leave unnamed
moves all else:
I cannot talk about love.

2   I am crippled: the midwife was my enemy.
These are my blessings,
my achievements by inaction.
I avoid no outcome.
I give life
but I do not possess my offspring.
I am supple.
I am the windbowed larch.

3   On lax velvet under aspenwood
I have no jade; I do not encourage thieves.
I hide from the people
the pelt of the sea-lynx:
I wish my friends to be humble.

4   Mark the delicacy of the moorhen's
quest under the willow bole.

To know the utter mildness
of my ways is to become like me.

5　The jawed stag beetle lacerates:
　　I do not save its victim.
　　My friends fall into nettlebeds:
　　I do not save my friends.

6　The cleft, the woman's withdrawing,
　　moves over all,
　　alien as the hawkmoth;
　　soft weblike the woman's way.
　　I turn again to the websoftness
　　and always find reception for my quest.

7　The queen bee,
　　bulbous with young, populates.
　　There is no desire in ivy;
　　it is drawn by the sun.
　　My body is not my building; it will last.

8　Morasses down, the water dwells,
　　moves in the lowest places.
　　There is kindness in my friendship,
　　there is truth in my talking,
　　there is ability in my art.
　　The plum falls only when the seed is near the skin.

9　Mark the thong's hum,
　　the force in the drawn ashbow.
　　Do a delicate thing,
　　then retire, go quietly and
　　move through dead vegetation:
　　gently do, gently go.

10 I wish to walk gently,
to achieve mildness.
I wish to love, not to interfere.
Move as a woman moves
between bedroom and childroom.
When you walk on the path
do not consider your sandals.

11 At the wheel's hub
the spokes sacrifice their names
and the wheel is named:
in the cup's hollow lies its use.

12 The eye dies from colour-glow,
the ear closes from music,
the tongue is wooden from pear-flesh.
I am free from the nightmares
of hawk, horse and hound:
I have courage to select.

13 You gave me an Indian tusk:
this disturbs me.
I am robbed, my tusk is stolen:
this also disturbs me.
The piebald badger makes no enemies,
makes no friends.

14 I see only water,
yet there is soundless life beneath it.
My ears strain, hear nothing.
My fingers grasp, and catch nothing.

I am haunted by the subtle woman-world:
I meet it and see no face,
I follow it and see no back.

15   I have no pride,
I need never change my views.
Pearls appear through the mudwhorl
by stillness.

16   I sit outside my own door
for four seasons.
I am tolerant of all weathers.
I see the leaf go back to the ground:
I am impartial to growth and death.

17   Finches, vipers and slime
wait in my friends' hearts.
The world moves, the world achieves.

18   When you spoke to me of love
I felt you knew nothing of it.
The path passes into ragwort:
the strivers came, judged, and gave names.
They overlooked two truths:
our enemies were once our friends,
competition is the death of mind.

19   I will burn the books
so my friends may speak clearly.
I will not speak of love

so that my friends may love.
I will recognise my friends
but I will not hail them in the street.

20 In spring the people
climb the terraces singing:
I have no home, I am idle.
In spring the people have plenty
yet they offer me nothing.
The people are learnèd:
I am confused, confined to a few books.

21 On the path alone are oak limbs.
To see the crow threaten
is to see strength.
The glasslike nymph of dragonfly
is vicious: I pass it by.

22 I cannot control life;
I am controlled.

23 In arguing
to agree is to end,
to end is to win.
I do not shout my name
yet my name is known.
I justify my actions only to superiors:
so far I have found only equals.

24 The globes, the cold globes,
    they do not last.
    I am like the globes, I am hail.
    Yet to leave the path is,
    with dunnock-wildness,
    to forsake the soul.

25 If I stand at the pinnacle, I do not stand.
    If I walk with ambition, I do not walk.
    The path is bridged by wicker
    from the stagnant pool:
    I sicken when I see this pool.

26 Out of the moist black bell I came:
    my first step drew scent from the lupins.
    Now my last step draws scent from the lupins:
    back to the moist black bell I go.

27 I move from town to town,
    never without supply.
    I am not taken by welcomes:
    I cannot smile, with so much to be done.

28 To be flippant is to lose control.

29 Such is my swiftness
    I do not mark the sea-flats.
    In my sea-house I never bolt the door,
    yet only my friends can enter.

I sit on the rocks
reclaiming all that is worthless,
all that is rejected.

30   I will walk manlike
and yet I will withdraw.
I stay here in my sea-house,
I do not go to the city to be praised.

31   The warmonger with horses
spreads his empire:
the world will not fall.

The uncoffined vase beneath the bones
cannot be improved.

32   I say to my friends not to strive.
Put down the shields and slings:
warmakers are locusts.
I say to my friends not to strive:
to raise an army is to clear the streets.
He who strives fights life.
He will not fight long.

33   I avoid in my walking the helmeted heads:
a victory is a burial.
The dead are worthless:
there is no skeletal beauty.

34 I cannot talk about friendship.
   Mark this carved talisman:

   it has beauty and yet has many uses.
   I go to my friend's house:
   I encounter no danger
   if I stay for the night.

35 To be helmeted is to be brutal,
   to self-fight is to be strong.
   If you touch me
   you will not go away giftless.

36 I am the sea-pool whence the myriads come.
   The snail wakes from under my rocks
   and moves on; I do not expect him to stay.
   Out of the moonpulled water I am a pool:
   at full tide I become the sea.
   I do not notice the change.

37 If you see in my hand
   earth as earth,
   then you will come to no harm.
   I hear songs in my room
   but see only ornaments.
   I am the mouth that swallows or spits out.

38 These towers you build,
   these pine-high towers,
   will fall stone from stone.
   There is none more silent than the mountains.

39 Much action comes
out of my mildness.

The fawn provokes all hands
to artistry.

40 I cannot speak of compassion
and if I speak I do not expect response.

I do not live so fragile
in the early pear-flower:
I live protected in the full pear.

41 Down from the rooftop,
inlaid with enamel
as waxen as laurel leaves,
my mosaic of a thousand
pieces of wood,
I can see my beams, my founding stones.

42 Out of the sea's shock
and swaying
into the whorl of his shell
the sea-snail returns.

43 Massive chords, the swell of woodwind,
all this is distantly music.
Yet when you hear of my mildness
you will laugh in my face,
proving my mildness.

44   On the sea-rock's side mica glints.
      On the sea-rock's side weeds smother.
      The dragon loneliness
      turns all from the streets:
      the man who tastes yew leaves
      will not leave the graveplace.

45   I have no form, no mole's claw,
      yet I penetrate the cleftless.
      I cannot speak,
      yet I pass on instruction.

46   Because I love so much
      I lose so much.
      My path passes intricate jade:
      I do not stop.
      Yet when I see the night coming
      I wait and take shelter:
      I am never in danger.

47   Whatever shape the gourd
      so shapes the water.
      I move my way into all circumstances.
      I am grey in summer
      to move among the lichens,
      in winter I am a silver fox.

48   I walk the path;
      my horses, horses of heart,
      bred supple and sinewy,
      pull ploughs of seasoned rootwood:

they do not bear armour.
Walks with the dragon loneliness too,
the dragon desire for possession.

49 Here on this cedar mountain
I do not leave my house.
Listening only to string music
I know where the path goes
and that 'know' is a corncrake evasion.

50 Yet I can tolerate losses:
I can lose everything.
When all has been lost
there is no action left,
and all is done by inaction.
Only when compelled to act
am I entirely abandoned.

51 Lie or be truthful,
I have no faculty of listening:
I do not take sides.
I am neither the king of cut teak
nor the black pawn:
I am the chessboard.

52 My eyes take meaning from art:
a corpse has eyes also.
I know what peace is:
no stone I overturn will be scorpioned.
I will not tread on vipers.

I will not be injured:
my utter mildness is my hidebound shield.

53   My path is my tent
against the minute spearhead sand,
my shield from the oak arrow.

I shall lead,
but I shall not command.

54   Out of my tumult
came artistry,
out of my tumult
the finished song.

55   My eyes are hawks;
I see the small things,
I see their utter mildness.

56   I walk on the path,
I do not consort with the sensual.
My friends are well fed,
my friends dress in green silk,
my friends wear white swords.

My friends are dying.

57   The otter grips until the bone breaks.
My sons will say these words
when I have long lain

between the two mountains.
They will talk of me
in the long nights.

58 I walk on the path.
I am frail but strong-gripped.
I have found no lasting consummation:
I can still dedicate myself.
I cry, but my daylong cries
never tell in my voice.

59 The swan,
the wordless swan,
sanctifies
water by its presence.

60 Yes, they have left fine temples —
but what language did they speak?

61 I speak: I change your ways.
Then I retire to my inner rooms:
there is no scroll, no flourish.
The opal does not glow
until unearthed.

62 I have suffered so long
and walked so much in travail
I have a limitless endurance.
The bone-tipped lash
arcs in the air.

63   Nothing comes to me at night
      that can terrify.
      Only he who steals from the grave
      is troubled by corpses.

64   Here is the woman-world:
      the fruited land is where
      the rivers come.
      My withdrawal and my friend's withdrawal
      leads to friendship.
      All I desire is a roof, a nightroof:
      let the night pass.

65   Without sound the brass god
      keeps to his altar.
      All my words, my workings, can be sold,
      my mildness can be cloaklike,
      silken but removable.
      When you have achieved
      shall I bow or call you friend?

66   My gravity foretells
      the greatest suffering.
      I enact it privately
      before it comes.
      I do not suffer greatly
      because I suffer in all my ways.

67   The shrew, frozen by eyes of ferret force,
      has no will to escape.
      I do not touch lest I spoil,

I do not strive lest I fail.
I read discarded manuscripts:
I give back to the world
what the people have ignored.

68 My endless rote of facts
    causes unrest among my friends.
    The lantern grates in the wind.

69 The people gather . . .
    wax masks and paper masks,
    music, shouts, and singing . . .
    they move through the city:
    they honour me.
    Yet I walk at the rear
    of the procession.

70 You ask me concerning this casket
    always in my possession . . .
    it holds three parchments
    saying in ink:
    'Love, ask little, do not strive.'
    I wish to see you preserved:
    I advise you to love.

71 So I mount in helmet
    and white steel,
    my shield encircling:
    yet in me there is no violence.
    There is peace;
    this is control over my friends.

72 No, lord, I will not give battle:
    let the people come and burn my house.

73 I speak clear words:
    but who will hear, who will practise?
    My songs have come from older songs.
    Unkempt I walk and no one beckons,
    no one raises his face.
    In this black rag in my hand
    is wrapped exquisite jade.

74 In my purse I take all my knowledge,
    inscribed on calf-cloth.

    Who steals my purse
    steals trash.

75 If my friends do not see
    the mildness of my ways
    they will encounter a greater mildness.
    I will not burn their houses,
    I will not mock their children.
    If you seek me
    do not look in high places.

76 If I take life I am brave,
    if I spare it I am also brave:
    the dragon misfortune stalks many.
    I do not ask, yet I am answered,
    I do not call, yet the people come.

77 Grass thrives wherever there is land:
    death is commonplace.
    I cannot threaten evil with death:
    it is not feared.

78 It is better to say nothing
    at all to my friends:
    it is a crime to interfere
    with their lives.

79 In life I see the yielding way:
    what is dead is not pliable.
    Women see beyond one life:
    they can exchange husbands.

80 The fox will kill nine grouse
    and eat one.

    I lead my friends,
    because I know their shame.

81 The tree, hollow and rain-rotted,
    holds the silver world of the wasp.

    I do not take sides
    because no hatred
    can be wholly dispelled.

82 I wish for this land
    not the words of love

but its actions:
love in action
is the white road
between the yew trees,
the exuberance of a girl
leaping from rock to rock.

83 In the shell's windings
the wind sounds like music.

Sikong Tu Walks in the Forest

from the Chinese of Sikong Tu, 837-908
based on his twenty-four poems on poetry

for Liam Brady

1

The soul that rests has riches:
death in motion, bourgeois man.
I walked along the wood-track
with an old knapsack of truths,
by deserts and by spring wells
with an old knapsack of truths.

2

Quietness of the high flight
of the solitary crane,
of rustles of a silk robe,
of coveted sweetnesses,
of elusive bamboo flutes:
a thing we cannot pocket.

3

Gathering green watercress,
I saw a beautiful girl,
willows, peach-trees, orioles,
reality, and such things:
I embraced those infinite
and those ancient miracles.

4

The green pines in the clear air,
I take off my cap and walk
under branches of birds' song.
No wild geese in the clear air,
but through the moonlit barriers
I could converse with my love.

5

And the god with lotus hands
passed, to the neighbouring moon:
Mount Hua shouldering the dark
and bronze silence from its bell.
I saw a lunar halo
around his calm lotus hands.

6

In rain a gentle cleric
writing his flower-poems.
Hints of birds in the bamboo,
his lute in a green twilight.
In rain a gentle cleric
still as a chrysanthemum.

7

'Take the iron from your heart;
contemplate familiar stars,
do not underrate the moon-

beam as a form of transport:
go back as light as child's steps
to your lunar yesterdays.

8

'Be vital as the rainbow
among the tall hills of Wu:
let the winds billow your silk;
keep Force as food in the soul;
create but do not grow less;
as the rainbow, give and live.

9

'If the mind has pearl inset,
what is gold to river mist,
to a branch of almond flowers,
to a painted bridge in mist,
to a friend at lute-music?
Simple things empearl the mind.

10

'Be wary of scrutiny,
of climbing mountains to look
down on birds, on waterfalls.
Do not climb up trees to see
a minute flower open.
Bow: it will be on the ground.

11

'All creation by your side,
the simple sun, moon and stars:
even a vagrant phoenix
and a tame leviathan.
God is not as far as Good:
open your palm, rain falls in.

12

'The poet can live outside
of print, but if his own song
cannot make him cry, if he
is not his first and finest
audience, then he merely
writes small words down on petals.

13

'That they might always come back
and be with us forever!
Bright river and bright parrot,
the stranger from the dark hill:
without the ash of writing,
may they always be with us!

14

'All words should be as things are:
artistic as flowers budding,
limpid as dew, important

as wide roads to horizons;
words should be as green as spring,
as like moonlight as is snow.

15

'I sit here under the pines
reading the old poetry,
heeding only day and dark,
unaware of the seasons,
happy, poor and literate:
an old man waiting for God.'

16

Confronted by such repose,
my mind quits its tenement
and walks after its love: she
glides like a jade figurine,
her greenness into the glade,
becoming the glade with light.

17

I climbed the T'ai-Hsing mountain
and I made a small echo.
The trees were like seas of jade,
flower-scent almost opaque:
I heard it rebound from the
waterfall, the same echo.

18

With plain words for simple thoughts
did I not touch the heart of
Tao? For I saw a poet,
a man with sticks on his back,
a man listening to music,
and I had not searched for them.

19

She whom I asked will not come
and I am bitter as death.
Centuries die in the glade
and Tao is passing away:
whom shall we ask salvation?
Wind whistles, leaf falls, rain falls.

20

I held his image inside,
like the image of all waves,
of all green things, all blossoms,
all the barrenness of hills.
To have likeness without form,
is that to possess the man?

21

I plunged arm up to elbow
in a pile of damp green moss,
in broken tendrils almost

found it: and found it almost
listening to the oriole.
Elusive as a rainbow!

22

Never about to be grasped:
like the white crane of Mount Hou,
like the white cloud of Mount Hua,
like vigour in old portraits
of the armed ancient heroes,
just about to be disclosed.

23

Life can be a hundred years:
drinking wine from fine goblets,
talking with our oldest friends,
visiting flower-gardens,
strolling with a staff of thorn —
but look at that great mountain!

24

I have made a simple song
walking now in the forest,
song of the Mighty Centre —
like pearls rolling on a floor?
Like turns of a water-wheel?
Explanations are for fools.

Catullus

from the Latin of Gaius Valerius Catullus, c.84-54 BC

for Eileen and Donal and Ronan

I

To whom am I to give my new and witty booklet,
smoothed off as it is with dry pumice-stone?
Cornelius, I give it to you; for you once considered
my scribbles worth something,
when you, with great daring, alone of Italians
decided to order the story of all of the ages
in three volumes (Good Lord!), learned and laboured at.
So take and keep this little booklet,
such as it is, whatever its worth is.

And oh, my virgin patroness,
may it last for more than one generation;
may it be durable.

II

Sparrow, my lady's pet, holding you in her lap,
it's *you* she plays with;
gives her fingertip for pecking
and makes you nip her sharply.
When she, my bright desire,
needs some pleasant pastime
(when her harsh passion dies)
she needs some small relief from sorrow.
And sparrow, if only I could play with you,
as my mistress does,
it would lighten all the cares
of my sad heart.

III

Mourn, Loves and Cupids,
and all men of refinement:
my lady's sparrow is dead,
the sparrow, my lady's pet,
whom she loved
more than she loved her own eyes.
For he was honey-sweet and knew her better
than any girl knows her mother.
He would not leave her lap
but hopping here and there
would chirp and chirp to his mistress only;
and now he goes the long dark journey
from where they say no one comes back.
My curse on you, cursèd Darkness
devouring all things beautiful;
you've taken away a lovely sparrow —
an evil deed, a small poor sparrow.
Because of you my girl's eyes
are puffed and red with sorrow.

V

Let us live, my Lesbia, and let us love;
let us value all the talk
of crabbèd me at one farthing.
Suns may set and rise again;
for us, once our short light is quenched,
there's but one night of perpetual sleeping.
Give me a thousand kisses,
then a hundred;
then another thousand, then a second hundred,
and then another thousand!

And then another hundred!
And when we have kissed
so many thousand times
we shall become confused
and we won't know the count.
Nor will any man, malicious,
give us the evil eye
because he won't be able either
to count our kisses.

VII

You ask, my Lesbia, how many kissings
would be enough for me?
As many as the number of the Libyan sands
that lie on Cyrene, dripping resin
between hot Jupiter's oracle
and old Battus' sacred tomb;
as many as the stars when night is still
and sees the furtive loves of men;
to kiss you so would be enough
(more than enough) for your mad Catullus;
to kiss so many kisses
that inquisitive eyes can't count
nor evil tongue bewitch.

LXX

My woman says there's none she'd rather marry
than I, not even if Jupiter himself came down and asked her.
So she says. But what a woman says to her eager lover
should be written on the wind and in rapid water.

LXXXVI

Quintia is beautiful to many; to me she's fair and tall
and steadfast. I acknowledge all these points.
But I totally deny she's beautiful; for she has no charm.
There's no spark of life in all her big body.
Lesbia *is* beautiful, for she has all that is most beautiful
and she has stolen all from all belovèds for herself alone.

XLIII

Hallo, young girl, whose nose is not so tiny,
who has neither black eyes nor a foot that's handsome,
nor a dry mouth, nor long fingers,
nor, indeed, an elegant way of speaking;
you girlfriend of a bankrupt from Formiae.
Is it you that are lovely as the province tells us?
Is it with you they compare my Lesbia?
Oh, this crude and tasteless era!

CIX

You promise to me, my life, that our loving
will be pleasant and last forever between us.
Great gods, grant that she'll be able to promise this truly;
that she, from her soul, may say it frankly
so that it is allowed to prolong through all our lives
this holy friendship, this everlasting contract.

LXXXVII

No woman can truly say she has been loved, my Lesbia,
 as much as you were loved by me;
in any contract no good faith was ever
 like that renewed by me, for love of you.

LXXXII

Quintus, if you wish Catullus to owe you his eyesight
or anything else, more costly than eyes are,
don't steal from him what he holds dearer than eyesight
or anything else that's even dearer than eyes are.

CIV

Do you believe that I was able to speak ill of my life,
 of her who is dearer to me than both my eyes are?
Nor would I, if able, be so miserably in love;
 but you and your friend exaggerate everything.

XL

Poor Ravidus, what badness of mind
drives you headlong into my iambics?
What god, ill-summoned by you,
is ready to stir up a row that is senseless?
Do you want to be known by the mouths of the mob?
What *do* you want? Notoriety, by whatever means?
Since you have wished to love my lady, you'll get it —
at the risk of a long-lasting punishment.

LXXVII

Rufus, I, being your friend, trusted you vainly
    and, indeed, at a great and disastrous price.
Is that how you robbed me, burning my entrails,
    tearing away every one of my blessings?
Alas, you tore them away; you're my life's cruel poison;
    you are, alas, a plague on my friendship.

XCI

Gellius, I hoped you would stand by me
    in this miserable, wretched love of mine.
Because I knew you well and thought you were loyal,
    thought you were able to keep your mind from dis-
        graceful infamy;
because I saw that she, whose great love was devouring me,
    was neither your mother nor your sister;
and as I was bound to you by much familiarity
    I thought that was reason enough for you.
But you thought it not enough; for you take such delight
    in any fault where there is something of misfortune.

CVII

If anything good ever happened to anyone eagerly longing
    and always unhopeful, it's a special pleasure to the mind.
And this is a pleasure to me, more precious than gold,
    that you give yourself back to me, Lesbia, who longed for
        you,
give yourself back to me, longing, yet always unhopeful.
    O omen, more bright than the day!

Is there anyone alive who is happier than I am?
    Who can say what in life is more desirable?

LXXIX

Lesbius is beautiful. And why not? Lesbia prefers him,
    Catullus, to you and all of your kindred;
if from three of his friends he could get kisses,
    this lovely boy would sell Catullus and all of his kindred.

XCII

Lesbia always speaks ill of me; she's never silent.
    May I die if she does not love me!
How do I know? Because I speak of her just as often,
        speak against her unceasingly.
    May I die indeed if I do not love *her*!

LXXXIII

Lesbia says many bad things to me in front of her husband
    and to that idiot causes great glee.
You mule, you understand nothing. If she forgot me, stayed
        silent,
    that would be rational; but because she snarls abuse at me
she not only remembers but (what's much more painful for
        her)
    she gets angry and so she prattles most passionately.

LI

He seems to me to be a god's equal.
He seems to rise above the gods — if that's allowed —
sitting opposite you and over and over he
   watches, and listens
to your sweet laugh, which, alas, takes away
all my senses; for as soon as I see you,
Lesbia, nothing is left of
   the voice in my mouth;
my tongue is numb and a thin flame
runs down through my limbs; my ears ring
with their own sound, my two eyes
   are covered in night.
Idleness, Catullus, is harmful;
you rejoice too much in idleness and frolicking;
Idleness has ruined, before now,
   both kings and blessèd cities.

LXXV

My mind has ruined itself by courtesy
   and is brought down to this, through your fault, Lesbia,
that it could not wish you well if you became the best of
   women
   or stop loving you if you did your worst.

LXXXV

I hate and I love. Why do I do this? Perhaps you will ask me.
I don't know. But I feel it. And I am in torment.

LXXII

You used to say once Catullus alone was known by you,
   Lesbia, and you'd not prefer Lord Jupiter to me.
I loved you then — not like commoners love their mistresses
   but as a father esteems his sons-in-law and sons.
But I know you know; and though I burn strongly
   more than ever now, I hold you cheaper and more fickle.
'How can this be?' you ask. Because such an injury as this
   makes your lover love you more but makes him think the
     less of you.

LX

Was it a lioness from the mountains of Libya
or a barking Scylla whose womb gave you birth?
You are so hateful, so hard-hearted;
you hold in contempt the voice of a supplicant in extremity.
Ah, too cruel-hearted!

LVIII

O Caelius, my Lesbia — that Lesbia,
Lesbia whom alone was loved by Catullus
more than himself and all that he had —
now at the crossroads and in the alleyways
robs the high-minded offspring of Remus.

XXXVII

You comrades of the lecherous tavern
nine doors from the pillar of Castor and Pollux,

do you think that you alone have dicks,
that you alone may thoroughly fuck all the girls
and think the rest of us just puck-goats?
Or because you sit in a queue impassively,
a hundred or two hundred, do you think
I wouldn't dare force a blow-job on the lot of you, sitting?
Think about it; for I'm going to scrawl
filthy graffiti about you on all the front of the inn
for the girl, who fled from my arms,
whom I loved as no one shall ever be loved,
for whom I fought great good fights,
has her practice there.
She is loved by all the good and prosperous men;
and, indeed, what is unworthy of her,
by all the puny adulterers and kerb-crawlers —
by you, especially, chief of the long-hairs,
Egnatius, son of rabbit-filled Spain,
made into a gent by a shady beard
and teeth rubbed clean by Spanish piss.

VIII

Poor Catullus, stop playing the fool.
Consider lost what you know is lost.
Once the days shone bright on you
when you followed where your girl led
(so loved by me, as none will ever love).
In those days so many joys occurred
which you desired and she did not;
bright for you were the days that truly shone.
Now she desires no more;
you should desire no more as well, you powerless man;
nor follow her who flees, nor live in misery;
but endure, make up your mind: be firm.

Farewell, my girl. Catullus *is* firm.
He will neither seek you out
nor entreat you against your will.
But you'll be sorry when no one calls on you.
Woe to you, you wicked wretch!
What kind of life have you left?
Who'll visit you now?
To whom will you seem pretty?
Who'll love you now? What name will you go by?
Who'll you kiss? Whose lips will you bite?
But you, Catullus, be resolved; be firm.

LXXVI

If pleasure awaits a man who, recalling past kindnesses,
    when he thinks he himself has been so devoted,
has broken no sacred trust, nor in any covenant
    has used the divine might of the gods to cheat anyone,
many joys, Catullus, in a long life, remain for you,
    because of this, your unrewarded love.
For whatever kindness a man can do anyone,
    by word or deed, has been done and said by you;
to an ungrateful heart this love was entrusted: it died.
    Why should you torment yourself further?
Why not be resolved in your mind, recouping your losses,
    no longer in misery, against the will of the gods?
It is hard to lay aside suddenly love long cherished;
    it is hard, but you should do it, any way you want.
This is your only safety, this must be your achievement;
    do it, whether it's possible or even impossible.
Oh gods, if you're merciful, or if to anyone
    you ever brought strength at the moment of death,
see me, in misery; if ever I wished for a life of purity,
    take from me this danger and this plague.

Alas, deep in my limbs steals a numbness inside of me
    which drives all happiness out of my heart.
That she should love me I pray no longer
    (for that's impossible), or that she turn chaste;
I want, myself, to recover and throw off this hateful
    sickness.
    Oh gods, grant me this, for all my devotion.

XI

Furius, Aurelius, Catullus' companions,
if even he passes through outermost India,
where the shore is made deaf by the far echo
    of eastern breakers,
or through Hyrcania or girlish Arabia,
or to the Scythians or Parthian bowmen,
or to the lands that the Nile darkens
    with its seven-fold delta;
or whether he crosses the high Alps when walking,
going to see the great Caesar's monuments,
the Rhine River in Gaul or Britons so dreaded —
    of men the remotest.
All these — and whatever the gods have decided —
we are steeled to encounter;
so then to my girl take this little message
    with not a good word in it:
let her live, let her prosper, with all her adulterers,
three hundred of whom all at once she embraces,
again and again (loving none of them truly),
    destroying their bollockses.
Let her not, as before, look around for my loving;
it was her own fault that it came to be fallen
like a flower at the edge of a meadow
    snipped by a plough in passing.

LXVIII^B

I cannot keep silent, goddesses,
about the way that Allius helped me,
and how much he helped by his services
lest time, that flies with forgetting ages,
bury in blind night that zeal of his;
but I will say to you, tell this to future thousands
and let this paper say when old:

. . . that dead he may become more known;
and don't let the spider who spins her high, thin web
do her work over Allius' forsaken name.
How that two-faced Venus gave me so much worry
you know, and the way she dried me up
when I was burning like Mount Etna
or the water of Thermopylae,
when my defected eyes did not stop
from wasting with continual tears
nor my cheeks from being wet with a shower of sorrow.
As at the top of a high mountain, a stream shines
and springs up from a mossy rock
and tumbles, rushing steeply down the valley,
crossing a densely peopled highway,
a sweet comfort to the tired and sweaty traveller;
and, as to sailors flung about by a black whirlpool,
comes a favourable wind, blowing more gently,
invoked by tears and prayers from Castor and from Pollox,
Allius was such a help to me.
He threw open a wide path through a closed-off field;
he gave me access to a house and my mistress
where we could make love together;
my shining goddess came there
with delicate feet, pressing the flashing soles
of her tapping sandals on the polished threshold,

as once to the house of Protesilaus
(a house begun in vain, since no victim's sacred blood
had pacified the lords of heaven)
came Laodamia burning with love for her husband.

Nemesis, may I never be rashly pleased
by what is suspect when the gods are unwilling.
How the hungry altar longs for holy blood
Laodamia learned, through the loss of her man;
forced to let go her arms from the neck of her husband
who, winter coming with its long nights,
should satisfy her eager love;
she would try to live if her husband was dragged from her
(which the Fates knew would happen shortly
if he went as a soldier to the walls of Troy).
For then, because of Helen's abduction,
Troy began to stir up the chief men of the Greeks
against herself. Troy! A monster!
You, common tomb of Europe and of Asia,
premature grave of men and all their courage,
brought death to my sad brother also —
oh, my brother taken from unhappy me!
Alas, joyful light, taken from your unhappy brother,
with you all my house is buried,
with you all my joys have perished
which your sweet love nourished while you lived;
now far away, and not among familiar tombs,
nor laid among the ashes of relations,
but buried in filthy Troy, in Troy the ill-omened;
an alien land holds you in foreign earth.
At that time, from everywhere,
the young men of Greece are said to have rushed there,
so that Paris, rejoicing in his abducted adulteress,
would not pass the time at leisure
in a peaceful bedroom.

And so, most beautiful Laodamia,
your husband, sweeter to you
than life or soul, was robbed from you,
and you were so swallowed in love's whirlwind
its raging carried you down a steep abyss
which in Arcadia, say the Greeks,
drains the marsh and dries up the fertile soil
which, it is said, was excavated,
the inside of the mountain cut out
by Heracles, the false-fathered,
when he struck down with sure arrow the monsters of
    Stymphalus
at the command of an inferior lord
so that more gods could use the door of Heaven
and that Hebe might not be long a virgin;
but your deep love was deeper than that gulf.
The head of the late-born grandchild his only daughter nurses
is not so dear to her father whose life is ending
but who just in time turned up
to have his name brought in to the witnessed will
for his grandfather's riches
and gets rid of the unnatural joy of a kinsman, now mocked,
and makes the vulture rise up from the grey head.
No dove delighted so much in its snow-white mate
that is always biting with its beak,
snatching kisses more insatiably
than a woman with lust brimming.
You alone, Laodamia, surpassed their passions
when, once, you were united with your blond-haired
    husband.
Just as worthy my bright one was, or little less,
when she came herself into my arms
and often Cupid ran around her
radiant in his saffron tunic.

And though she's not content with just Catullus
I will bear the few faults of my modest lady,
lest we become as irksome as jealous fools are.
Juno too, greatest of those who live in heaven,
has often contained her anger over her husband's faults
as she learns of the many misdeeds of insatiable Jupiter;
and yet it's not reasonable to compare men with gods.

. . . So away with this thankless burden of an anxious father.
For she did not come to me led by his right hand
to a house fragrant with Assyrian perfume,
but gave me in the wondrous night small stolen gifts
taken away from the very arms of her husband.
So it's enough if to me alone the day is granted
which she makes bright with a white stone.

This gift (all I could do), made in verse, is sent to you,
Allius, for many kind services;
lest this day, that day, and another and another
should touch your name with corroded rust.
To this the gods will add many more, which Themis once
used give in ancient time to pious men.

May you be happy, you, your life, your lady
and your house, the house in which we sported;
may he, who first gave you to me, be happy,
from whom all good things sprung for me;
and she above all, who is dearer to me than myself —
my light who, living, makes it sweet for me to live.

The Hag of Beare

from the Old Irish (9th century), anonymous

The woman of Beare sang this when old:

As to the sea laps low tide
    to me falls fading of age;
    grief for myself at fading,
    greed in the teeth of my days.

I am Buí, the hag of Beare,
    I wore an eternal gown;
    but I am naked today
    of even a cast-off shroud.

Money was all you loved,
    and not people;
    but we, while we were alive,
    our love was for the people —

for we loved the peopled plains
    we rode, and we loved our hosts;
    hospitable, good, they made
    of no giving a long boast.

Today you claim all, yet you
    grant none nothing: if you give
    you shame the given with great
    boasting of a little gift.

Now my body, bitter, finds
    the corridors of final
    recognition, the gaze of
    God in his own possession.

Now my hands, wrinkled to long
    bones, hang down dead, hands that locked
    kings of this land in loving,
    in the old days, my lost days.

O hands, wrinkled to long bones,
    even at my odd hours of lust
    I must tell young men begone
    should they come. I have no love.

The bodies of young women
    bound as rabbits in springtime.
    I only regret. *I* am
    a barren unloved woman —

for my tongue hides no honey
    and I look to no wedlock;
    white what is left of my hair
    hidden under a hag's cloak.

Not the old I envy:
    they die; but youth
    and monuments both assailed
    as I am, and they still hold.

Winter makes war with the waves;
    today no king will come here,
    nor the lowest road-walker.
    I expect no one today.

I know what they are doing,
    liquid horses of the sea;
    spaced far in their maned groups,
    they gallop away from me.

By loving
    I wasted my self to age,
    but beauty leaves me alone:
    I am old, and no lust stays.

When the sun
    beats a haze of hotness from
    the sea, so yet I must go
    clothed. I am spent, and old.

And yet to waste by loving
    is no waste: for I am glad
    I was made old by pleasure,
    I am glad my flesh was glad.

Green to grass comes back each spring;
    I am eternally old.
    Each acorn gives way to earth,
    bright tables fall to bare boards.

Past, in my days of firm breasts,
    wine was my drink and sweet words
    my food, tall men my lovers;
    now curds, sour as my own milk.

Beneath my cloak my skin hides,
    grained with age and unlovely;
    a white hair covers my skin
    like fungus on a dead tree.

Robbed of me my blue right eye,
    lent for land I own forever;
    and robbed of me my left eye
    secures it, mine forever.

The three floods
    in which I would dream to drown:
    a flood of loves, of horses
    and of gentle slim grey hounds.

O birth-wave,
    death-wave, you bore, you broke me;
    you, last, I will know your face
    when you must come to take me.

O death-wave,
    though great, my friends in darkness
    are — yet come and make your use
    of me. I never refuse.

Well for the islands to which
    again the flood-waves come: now
    I, alone on my ebbed beach,
    I know no face nor no house.

Marbán, a Hermit, Speaks

from the Old Irish (9th century), anonymous

For I inhabit a wood,
　　unknown but to my God,
my house of hazel and ash
　　as an old hut in a rath.

And my house small, not too small,
　　is always accessible;
women disguised as blackbirds
　　talk their words from its gable.

The stags erupt from rivers,
　　brown mountains tell the distance;
I am glad as poor as this
　　even in men's absence.

Death-green of yew,
huge green of oak
　　sanctify,
and apples grow
close by new nuts;
　　water hides.

　　　　Young of all things,
　　　　bring faith to me,
　　　　　　guard my door:
　　　　the rough, unloved
　　　　wild dogs, tall deer,
　　　　　　quiet does.

Marbán, brother of Guaire, King of Connacht (7th century), forsook the life of a warrior-prince and became a hermit. His brother tried to persuade him to return to the courts and this was his answer.

In small tame bands
the badgers are,
    grey, outside;
and foxes dance
before my door
    all the night.

All at evening
the day's first meal
    since dawn's bread:
trapped trout, sweet sloes
and honey, haws,
    beer and herbs.

Moans, movements of
silver-breasted
    birds rouse me,
pigeons perhaps.
And a thrush sings
    constantly.

Black-winged beetles
boom, and small bees;
    November
through the lone geese
a wild winter
    music stirs.

Come fine white gulls
all sea-singing,
    and, less sad,
lost in heather,
the grouses' song,
    little sad.

For music I
have pines, my tall
 music-pines:
so who can I
envy here, my
 gentle Christ?

'Calling bell . . .'

from the Old Irish (9th century), anonymous

Calling bell
brought here by wild wind nightly:
I would contest your clarion
rather than war with women.

'He is my love . . .'

from the Middle Irish, anonymous

He is my love,
   my sweet nutgrove:
a boy he is —
   for him a kiss.

'Eve, I, wife to the first man . . .'

from the Middle Irish (11th century), anonymous

Eve, I, wife to the first man,
   and I, Eve, the rage of Christ,
mine robbed of prize by my own hand:
   I should have been crucified.

As of a king my domain,
   but broke to shame by my choice;
as of Satan my damning,
   my limbs no longer joyful.

I ate the apple, Eve, I.
   And past me my greed coursed
and so, as long as alive,
   all my kind will be perverse.

But for me, where would ice kill?
   Now the shining winter seals,
now is sadness, now is hell,
   fear, as well: because of me.

'Have mercy on me, O Trinity . . .'

from the Irish of Giolla Brighde Mac Con Midhe,
died before 1281

Have mercy on me, O Trinity,
    who put sight in the eye of the blind
(and, harder still, pushed grass through granite);
    do not leave me without a child.

You put blossoms on trees, great Father
    (I desperately try to understand);
having made the trees to blossom
    would giving me children be more hard?

Ear of wheat from blade, oak from acorn grows,
    slim seedling from a grain —
beautiful bright miracles these;
    surely one child would be no great strain?

Salmon in every speck of roe, bird in egg
    (these I can barely grasp);
or a hazel-nut in its shell —
    but no child on my wife's lap?

You deceived me with beautiful children;
    I saw them flower to no avail;
have pity on me, Creator;
    consider my childless state.

An empty household, for an active man,
    is a great cause of grief;
send just *one* child to our house —
    Holy Virgin, Mary, send relief.

People without progeny, though prosperous,
    are only heard of while alive;
beauty without good fortune is fine —
    but it's a grain of seed that does not thrive.

There is no lasting Hell
    except the Hell of having no child;
bare stones in wild fields of grass
    those who leave no children behind.

'Ach! this new Irish fashion and ach! . . .'

from the Irish (17th century),
?Brian Mac Giolla Phádraig, c.1585–1653

Ach! this new Irish fashion and ach!
beggar-women's sons with long curly locks,
bright cuffs on their wrists and big showy rings —
like any pure-blooded Irish prince.

Each bum and his son to their chins in starch,
with gaiters on and thrown-back scarves,
pipes of tobacco in their gobs a-puff,
from wrist to elbow all braceleted up.

The snare that tripped me was Life, that fickle trickster;
there's respect in each house for a man with broken English
and no nod at all to the man with a poet's training
but 'piss off now, you and your perfect Gaelic!'

'On getting up one morning . . .'

from the Irish (17th century or later), anonymous

On getting up one morning
the summer sun was shining;
I heard the hounds all baying,
    and the sweet song of the birds.
Badgers, all small creatures,
with their long beaks the woodcocks,
noises from the echoes,
    shooting of heavy guns;

the red fox on the boulder,
a thousand shouts from riders,
a sad woman on the roadway
    counting her few geese.
Now they're cutting down the forests
we will go out of the harbour,
and, Seán Ó Duibhir an Ghleanna,
    you have no game.

That is my lingering sorrow,
shade for my head demolished,
perished by the north wind,
    and death is in the sky;
my happy hounds being tied up,
not allowed to bay or gambol —
they'd take sorrow from the children
    in the bright noon of day.

On the rock, beloved by gentry,
stags, nimble, proud and antlered,
who'd move among furze bushes
    till the last day of the world;
if I get peace for just a moment
from the 'good people' of this parish

I will make my way to Galway
   and leave behind all joy.

The townlands of Glownatruha,
their people have no prop nor leader;
in the street of drinking vessels
   they no longer toast 'long life';
and I have no luck nor shelter
from Cloone to Stooknagolm
and the hare upon the headland
   wanders at his ease.

Why this attack by Saxons,
beating, slashing, flaying?
The sweet thrush and the blackbird
   sing no fine songs in the trees;
a great omen for more warfare,
the clergy scourged, and people
being sent to desert places
   in the mountain glens.

Last Lines

from the Irish of Dáibhí Ó Bruadair, 1625-1698

Though I must suffer now the world's bitter lash
that this year down upon my head will crash,
it was not fractured language tore my self-control apart.
I lacked the trash that would have trivialized my craft.

I have no time or strength for friendships now,
since my belovèd people have left the south.
The much-missed men that I lament about
were not at risk from the poems of my mouth.

Lament for Tadhg Cronin's Children

based on a poem by Aodhagán Ó Rathaille, c.1670-1729

That day the sails of the ship were torn
and a fog obscured the lawns.
In the whitewashed house the music stopped.
A spark jumped up at the gables
and the silk quilts on the bed caught fire.
They cry without tears —
their hearts cry —
for the three dead children.

Christ God neglect them not
nor leave them in the ground!

They were ears of corn!
They were apples!
They were three harpstrings!
And now their limbs lie underground
and the black beetle walks across their faces.
I, too, cry without tears —
my heart cries —
for the three dead children.

Carraig na bhFear

from the Irish of Seán Ó Murchú na Ráithíneach, 1700-1762

If sometimes I take up my pipes
they say, 'He will fail at all trades —
'twould be better for him to push spades
and then he'd be full of God's grace!'

Well, I know enough clever tricks —
my work attention won't lack:
but I'll never part with my music —
I can't live without sport or the crack!

No blame for my likes to be active —
the musicians and poets I rule;
I won't part with my friends over tillage —
do you think I'm some kind of fool?

It's not a disgrace for the young
to be manly, obliging and polite —
to straighten them out with a tune
robs no one of money or life.

I think it is better for me
to follow up fun every day
than surly, degenerate woes
and unmannerly, ignorant ways.

Don't let the thick stiff-necks declare
that I am a man with no plan —
so? I love a big crowd far too much
and alone I'm a sorrowful man.

When a storm comes blowing around
or it happens it's some good saint's day

I talk for a while about poems
and the lore of each subtle sage.

When I think the company's full up
with too much learning and lays,
I'll eagerly take my pipes with me
and tune them ready to play.

Beside a fireplace of ashes
from there I'll seldom be gone
and a crowd will come round for to hear me —
a lonesome journey for none.

Learning and music are enemies still
of all dreary pigs in this life;
fun, out of spite, they won't tolerate —
against them I will carry the fight.

All their wars mean nothing to me
or whether they go or come —
I will never go looking for them
whether I'm empty or full.

I never praise nor fault my gifts
but I once told the world with a shout
that I do not flinch from being merry and kind
since they're the gifts that God gave out!

They sleep without joy in the cinders,
these gloomy and gluttonous boars —
no luck or no light in their windows
while I'm all good manners and show.

I ask of good Mary and Christ
that that person forever may fall

who abandons the fun and crack
for works that don't need him at all.

The curse on them of Art mac Cuinn
through whom the Fianna were defeated
(that gang hate curses cast like this —
like Art, they're treacherous and cheaters).

With love and reverence for me,
all of these lines rehearse:
Seán Ó Murchú, he was the source
of this eminently readable verse.

O'Sullivan's Malediction

from the Irish of Eoghan Rua Ó Súilleabháin, 1748-1784

Oh acute and honest poet who reads the old authors,
as you can solve quickly all difficult questions;
tell us out plain, after weighing your answers,
will the Irish be long in the power of the foreigners?

'Tis not fine recitation nor perusing old writers,
nor the speed of the light-footed warriors,
will scatter the foreigners all out of Ireland
but the power of the Lord when he justly destroys them.

Gibson, Brown, Townsend, Gibbs, Tonson and Gore,
Dixon, Knowles, Boulton, Bullen and Bowen;
Wrixon, Southwell, Moulton, Miller and Dore —
starvation and jail to what remains of their spawn.

Southwell, Steelman, Stephens, Stannard and Swain,
Furnell, Fleetwood, Reever, Chapman and Lane;
every hangman, proud, swarthy and bald, of their race
in a battle of bullets may they be defeated and slain.

Lysaght, Leader, Clayton, Compton and Coote,
Ivers, Damer, Batemen, Bagwell and Brooks;
Ryder, Taylor, Maynard, Marrick and Moore —
may the strong tribes of Cashel undo all these boors.

Upton, Evans, Bevan, Bassett and Blair,
Burton, Beecher, Wheeler, Farren and Phair;
Turner, Yielding, Reeves and Waller and Deane —
Cromwell and his gang, may their herd be scattered astray.

Oh lovely God, oh Jesus, oh Father of the Lamb,
who sees us in fetters and severely in bonds;
King of Heaven, Protector, answer my song:
destroy, and dispel these lice from our land.

The Connerys

from the Irish (19th century), anonymous

Oh Comyn, hear my curse, may God's judgement be much
      worse
    upon that final day.
May he rot the guts of that pack of scuts
    that you have in your pay.
Oh they swore their oaths in their lying throats
    so that you could have your way.
And so you sent the Connerys far across the seas,
    all the way to the New South Wales.

Oh the man who took the stand and thought he'd try his hand
    to help and plead our case —
From the early dawn he stood all alone
    till nine o'clock that day.
Oh the earth it shook when the oaths were took
    and falsely he did swear —
God love that poor old man for his soul is surely damned —
    or so the clergy say.

Our jackets are being cut, our britches being made up,
    our convict clothes prepared —
Oh sea-going clothes as you well know
    we never used to wear.
If our friends can't help they will crack our necks
    and we'll be in quicklime laid.
Unless we're shipped away to spend a term of days
    far away in the New South Wales.

Oh blessèd queen of men and heaven's own bright king,
    Oh bring us peace and ease,
And help the nurse who cries after us
    at home in sad dismay.

Oh during the holy Mass both beg and ask,
 and almighty God do pray
To bring the Connerys from far across the seas
 back home from the New South Wales.

Heine

from the German of Heinrich Heine, 1797-1856

Gesanglos war ich und beklommen
So lange Zeit — nun dicht ich wieder!
Wie Tränen, die uns plötzlich kommen,
So kommen plötzlich auch die Lieder.
                    — Neue Gedichte, 1844

Songless, anxious, a long time —
now I am writing again!
Suddenly songs come upon us,
like tears, like pain.

1

My gold-haired beauty,
you, I believe, I see
every morning in the gardens
under the chestnut trees.

Every day she walks
with two old crones.
Are they her aunts beside her
or dragons dressed in clothes?

2

Why I really created the world?
I'll gladly make it known to all.
I felt in my soul, burning
like flames of frenzy, the Call.

Sickness was really the reason —
to create I was impelled.
By creating I could recover,
by creating I got well.

3

We felt very deeply for each other
and, strange to tell,
we got on very well.
We often played at 'Husband and Wife'
and, strange to tell,
we did not bicker, did not fight;
our jokes we happily shared,
we kissed and we embraced.

And in the end, with young delight,
we played 'Hide and Seek' in wood and lane;
we became so good at going ahide
that we never found each other again.

4

In their dark eyes there are no tears,
they sit at their looms and bare their teeth.
'Germany, we weave your winding-sheet;
into it a curse we weave.
We are weaving, weaving.

'A curse on the God to whom we prayed
in winter's cold, in hungry days;
in vain we hope, in vain we wait —

we are deluded and betrayed,
but we are weaving, weaving.

'A curse on the King, the rich man's King,
he could no ease to our misery bring;
our last penny from us he robbed
and left us to be shot down like dogs,
but we are weaving, weaving.

'A curse on our false Fatherland
where only insult and disgrace can flourish;
where every flower is soon bent down
and by decay the worm is nourished.
And we are weaving, weaving.

'Our shuttles fly, our looms make noise,
we're busily weaving, day and night.
Old Germany, we weave your winding-sheet
and into it our curse we weave.
We are weaving, weaving.'

5

I do not believe in the Heaven
which the priestling indites;
I only believe in your eyes,
they are my heavenly light.

I do not believe in that Lord God
whom the priestling indites;
I only believe in your soul —
no other God have I.

I do not believe in the Evil One,
in Hell, or in Hell's smart;
I only believe in your eyes
and in your evil heart.

6

And the *castrati* complained
when I raised my loud note;
they complained and said
what I sang was too coarse.

And each one of them sang
with a small, sweet voice;
their trills, like crystal rang
so fine, so nice.

They so sang of Love's longing,
of Love and Love flowing free,
that the ladies swam in tears
at such artistry.

7 IT GOES OUT

The curtain falls, the play is done.
People leave the auditorium.
'Did they like the play?' I wonder.
I think I hear their clapping thunder.

The highly respected audience
thankfully applauds the writer.
But now the house is *plein de silence*,
joy and lights less brighter.

A dull, discordant sound
not far from the deserted stage
is echoing
perhaps a worn string breaking
on an old violin.

Peevish, in the stalls,
rats scratch here and there;
the whole place smells of rancid paraffin.
The last lamp groans,
sputters in despair
and then gives in.
That last lamp's groan,
that last poor light
was my soul.

8 THE ANGELS

Really, as a doubting Thomas,
I do not believe in the 'Heaven'
which the doctrines of the Catholics
and the Hebrews take as given.

But as to whether angels
might not be, or might —
of this I have no doubt:
the spotless creatures of the Light
on Earth still walk about.

But, Madam, that they have wings:
this I do deny.
Many have seen flightless angels;
so have I.

Lovingly, with white hands,
lovingly, with lovely eyes,
they protect all men
and turn bad luck aside.

Their grace and favour
comfort everyone,
especially the tormented man
who carries a double load,
especially the one
that people call a poet.

9

Well, chaps,
I have decided
to go off the schnapps.
I know I'll be derided
('you *know* — a slight lapse').

But I have spoken
to my *Hofweltweiser*
(a very sound adviser —
but you know the way he yaps);
he said (being older and much wiser):
'Vows are made, vows are broken.'

And at this stage, as God well knows,
I had to interpose
and asked:
'Will you and all your wisdom
get me off the schnapps?'

So he stroked his ancient brow
and he said,
'My son, well now . . .
of course you'll give it up . . .
well, you *will* . . . *perhaps.*'

10

My father was one of those dried-up chaps,
a stubborn auld louser;
but I, when I have drunk my schnapps,
I become a Kaiser!

It's a magic drink, perhaps;
it revives my mental powers;
as soon as I have drunk my schnapps
China bursts into flowers!

The Middle Kingdom thinks it can
become a field of flowers run wild,
and I, I almost become a man —
and my wife's with child!

There is abundance everywhere,
the sick get well again;
Confuse-us, my pet philosopher,
has clear thoughts in his brain.

The black bread of my soldiers
turns into almond-cake;
all tramps inside my borders
in silk and satin traipse.

My Mandarins, malingerers,
Freemasons to a man,
win back their youthful vigour
and make their pigtails dance.

The great Pagoda's ready
(please pass the flagon);
the last of the Jews will be baptised
and get the Order of the Dragon.

Gone is the spirit of Revolution.
The high-born Manchus shout,
'We don't want a Constitution!
Bring back the cat, the birch, the knout!'

The doctors tell us not to lapse,
advise against intoxication;
I, however, down my schnapps
and drink to the health of the nation!

Another schnapps and another schnapps!
It tastes like pure Manna.
My happy people's minds collapse
and still they roar 'Hosannah!'

Gypsy Ballads

after the Spanish of Federico García Lorca, 1898-1936

BALLAD OF THE MOON

The moon comes into the forge
in her dress of hoop and flower.
The child stares, stares at her:
the child is staring at *her*.
The moon moves her arms
in the agitated air,
exposes breasts of hard tin,
voluptuous and pure.
'Run away, moon, moon, moon!
for if the gypsies arrive
they will make of your heart
necklets and rings of white.'
'Child, let me dance, dance!
When the gypsies arrive
they will find you on the anvil
closing your eyes.'
'Run away, moon, moon, moon!
for now I hear their horses.'
'Child, leave alone: do not step
on my starched whiteness.'
The horseman was coming nearer!
Drumming the tambourine plain!
Inside the forge, the child
had closed her eyes again.

A bronze dream, they came
along the olive groves,
their heads held high,
their eyes half closed.

Listen — the bird of night sings,
sings, sings in the tree. And
the moon moves through the sky
with a child by the hand.

Inside the forge
the gypsies shout and weep.
The breeze watches, watches.
All is watched by the breeze.

PRECIOSA AND THE WIND

Swishing her parchment moon
Preciosa sweeps
along an amphibious path
of crystals and laurel-leaves.
The silence without stars
runs from her swishing
and falls where sea beats and sings
in its night full of fishes.
Guarding the white towers
on the mountain peak
where the English people live
the Customs men sleep.
The water gypsies raise —
just to pass the time —
spiralling roundabouts
and branches of green pine.
Swishing her parchment moon
swift Preciosa sweeps.
The wind sees her and rises,
the wind which does not sleep.
A naked St Christopher
fingers a sweet unreal pipe
and darting many heavenly tongues
he watches her go by.
'Girl, let me lift up your dress,
let me examine you:
open to my ancient fingers
the blue rose of your womb.'

And while she tells her story
and sits crying there
she throws away her tambourine,
and as she madly goes

the male wind chases her
with his hot sword.
The olive trees turn pale,
the sea draws in its moans:
flutes in shady places sing
and the smooth gong of snow.
Run, Preciosa, run!
for the green wind will get you!
Run, Preciosa, run!
Look, here he comes,
satyr of setting stars
with his shining tongues!

A frightened Preciosa
runs to the high pines
and goes into the house
where the English Consul lies.
Woken by her screams
the Customs men come down,
their black cloaks close-fitting
and their caps up on their brows.
The English man gives to her
a tumbler of lukewarm milk
and offers her a glass of gin
which she does not drink.
Outside, on the tiles of slate,
the wind snaps his teeth in rage.

THE FIGHT

At the bottom of the hill
lie open knife-blades,
they shine like fishes,
beautiful with blood.
Light outlines like cards
in the sharp green places
the panicking of horses,
the panic on horsemen's faces.
On the branches of the olive
two old women wail.
The bull of the fight
is pawing at the wall.
Black angels bring
cloths of water and of snow:
with huge wings like blades
the black angels go.
The gypsy from Montilla
rolls down the slope dead,
his body pregnant with lilies
love-apples in his head.

The judge with his Civil Guards
comes through the olive-grove,
like silent songs of snakes
a trail of blood moans.

The evening, mad with fig trees
and warm sounds,
falls exhausted on
the horsemen's thigh-wounds.
Through the air of sundown

black angels fly,
angels with long hair
and hearts of olive oil.

THE SLEEPWALKING BALLAD

Green, how I love you, green.
Green wind, green branches.
Ship up on the sea,
horse in the mountain ranches.
With shadows at her waist
she dreams at her balcony window,
green flesh, green hair
and eyes of cold silver.
Green, how I love you, green.
Huge stars of frost
come out with the fish-shadow
to open the dawn's pass.
The fig tree strokes the wind
with its sandpaper talons,
the thieving cat of a mountain
bristles its sour aloes.
But who will come? And from where?
She lingers on the balcony,
green flesh, green hair,
dreaming of the bitter sea.

'Friend, I want to swap
my saddle for your mirror,
my horse for your house,
my knife for your bed-cover.
Friend, I have come bleeding
from the passes of Cabra.'
'If I could, young man,
I would close the bargain.
But I am no longer myself
nor is my house my own.'
'Friend, I wish to die
decently at home

with white linen bed-clothes.
Do you not see this wound
I have from breast to throat?'
'On your white shirt you have
three hundred dark roses.
Your blood smells pungent
as through your sash it oozes.
But I am no longer myself
nor is my house my own.'
'At least let me climb up
to the high balcony alone,
let me climb, let me up
to the green balconies
where the water sounds
on the moon's many balconies.'

And now the two friends climb
up to the green stairs,
leaving a trail of blood,
leaving a trail of tears.
Small lanterns of tin
on the roofs quaked:
a thousand drums of crystal
wounded the daybreak.
Green, how I love you, green.
Green wind, green branches.
The two friends climb
and the strong wind launches
a strange taste in the mouth,
mint, gall and basil.
'Friend, where is she? Tell me,
where is your bitter girl?
How often she waited for you!
How often she would wait

on this green balcony,
cool face, black hair.'

Over the face of the well
the gypsy girl shivered,
green flesh, green hair
and eyes of cold silver.
An icicle of the moon
over the water held her:
the night became as secret
as a little square.
Green, how I love you, green.
Green wind, green branches.
Ship up on the sea,
horse in the mountain ranches.

THE GYPSY NUN

Flowers in the bursting reeds.
Silence of myrtle and chalk.
A nun embroiders blossoms
on straw-coloured cloth.
In the grey chandelier
seven birds of the prism flock:
a church growls in the distance
like a bear upon its back.
She sews gracefully and well
but would prefer to show
her own fantastic flowers
on cloth the colour of straw.
Sunflowers and magnolias,
sequins and satin bows,
saffrons and strange moons
on the altar-cloth she sews.
In the nearby kitchen
oranges become ripe:
flowers from Almería,
the five wounds of Christ.
Inside the nun's eyes
two handsome bandits ride:
her black breast-cloth swells
with a dormant, final sigh.
As she sees the clouds and hills
at the empty plains' edge
she breaks her desolate heart
of sugar and sweet herbs.
And vertical light dances
on the window-lattice for hours,
making a high chessboard . . .
she lingers with her flowers.

THE UNFAITHFUL WIFE

And I took her to the river
believing she was single
but she had a husband . . .

It was the night of Santiago
and, as if in duty bound,
as the crickets flared up
the streetlamps died down.
At the last street corners
I touched her sleeping breasts
and they opened to me swiftly
like spikes of hyacinth.
The starch of her petticoats
sounded in my ears
like long pieces of silk
cut by sharp shears.
The treetops grew enormous
without their light of silver
and a horizon of dogs
barked very far from the river.

Past brambles, reeds and thorntrees
I took her by the hand.
Under her clustered locks of hair
I made a hollow in the sand.
Neither flower nor shell
had a skin so fine,
nor with such brilliance
did moon-mirrors shine.

Like frightened fish
they slipped from me, her thighs:

one full of cold,
the other full of fire.
On the best highway
that night I was riding,
saddling a mare of mother-of-pearl
without stirrups or bridle.

Smeared with sand and kisses
I took her from the river
and the air above us battled
the swords of the lily.

Then I behaved as I am,
a true gypsy after all:
I gave her a sewing-basket
of satin the colour of straw.

BALLAD OF THE BLACK SORROW

The beaks of cockerels
dig in search of dawn
when Soledad Montoya
from the dark hill comes down,
scent of horse and shadow
upon her copper flesh
and songs wail around
the smoky anvils of her breasts.

'Soledad of my sorrow,
the horse that runs away
will find the sea at last
and be swallowed by the waves.'

'Do not remind me of the sea
for a black sorrow grieves
in the land of the olives
beneath the whisper of the leaves.'

'Soledad of pitiful sorrow,
the saddest of all women,
sour with always waiting
you weep tears of lemon.'

'Mad in my sorrow
I pace from door to door,
my long unbound hair
trailing across the floor.

'My flesh and my clothes
turn as black as jet,
my petticoats of linen,
my thighs of poppy red.'

'Soledad, wash your body
with water of the skylark:
Soledad Montoya,
give peace to your heart.'

Whirl of sky and leaf.
Down below the river sings.
With flowers of the pumpkin
day its daylight rings.

O sorrow of the gypsies,
always pure and always alone!
O sorrow of the hidden ways,
sorrow of the distant dawn!

SAN MIGUEL

They step along the ledges
down from the mountain peak,
mules and shadows of mules
laden with sunflower seeds.
Their eyes in the shade
are blurred, with immense night.
The knotted, plaited breeze
rustles the brackish light.
A sky of white mules
closes its quicksilver eyes
and gives to the still shade
a heart-stopping quiet.
The water makes itself cold
so that none may drink:
the water, wild and hatless,
jumps from the mountain's brink.
In the alcoves of his tower
surrounded by his lamps
St Michael, masked in lace,
shows his lovely flanks.
This homely archangel
a gentle pretence plays,
assuming a sweet anger
of feathers and nightingales.
St Michael sings in the windows,
priests of the uncounted hours,
fragrant with eau-de-cologne
perfumed with strange flowers.

The sea is dancing on the beach
to a poem of balustrades,
the edges of the moon
lose reeds and win refrains.

Eating their sunflower seeds
the flashy girls come:
like huge planets of copper
sway their hidden bums.
And tall horsemen come
and ladies of sad gait,
rose-dark with nostalgia
for lost nightingales.
And the Bishop of Manila,
poor and blind from saffron,
for the riders and their ladies
an ambiguous Mass is offering.

In the alcove of his tower
St Michael quietly lurks,
his petticoats coagulate
with sequined needlework.

SAN RAFAEL

1

Closed coaches come nearer
the ready rain-courses
where the water polishes
a naked Roman torso.
The river reflects
the coaches in its ancient glass
between sheets of flowers:
singing clouds pass.
And children weave and sing
the disillusion of this place
around the ancient coaches
lost on the dark highways.
And under this haunted awe
Cordoba does not quake,
for if a shadow lifts
her artifacts of smoke
a foot of marble steps span
her splendid slim soul.
Above the arch of triumph
cheering the winds grey
petals of silver alloy
are on glittering display,
and while the bridge echoes
sound from undersea halls
the sellers of tobacco
escape across the broken wall.

2

A single fish in the water
joins Cordoba of the reeds
onto another Cordoba —
Cordoba of planned streets.
While on the bank disrobe
children of impassive face,
students of Tobias
and warlocks at the waists.
And they annoy the fish
with ironic questionings:
whether it wants flowers of wine
or a dive through the moon's ring?
But this fish which gilds the pool
and the marble bottom
teaches them to see the poise
of a single column
and the alcoved archangel,
dark in his moorish sequins,
in this gathering of waves
looks for cradles and soft speaking.

A single fish in the water
joins Cordoba of the reeds
onto that other Cordoba —
Cordoba of man-made streets.

GABRIEL

1

A handsome young man —
waist slim, shoulders wide,
large eyes and sad mouth:
skin like apples at night,
and nerves of fiery silver —
walks the deserted street.
His patent-leather shoes
crush air-like dahlias underneath,
in two rhythms which make
brief celestial songs.
On the sea shore
there is no lovelier palm frond,
no finer emperor crowned,
no lovelier lost star.
When over his jasper breast
his fine head fell
the night sought open spaces
because it wished to kneel.
And all the guitars sang
for Gabriel alone,
tamer of white moths,
hater of willow groves.

2

A gypsy girl,
in moonlight badly clad,
opened her door to the star
that was coming down the road.
Gabriel the angel

with a lily and a smile,
child of the moorish tower,
had come to visit a while.

In his embroidered waistcoat
hid crickets palpitate:
the stars of the night
become bells and vibrate.
'Gabriel, I am here
with the three nails of joy,
your radiance unfolds
jasmines in my eyes.'
'God bless you, girl,
dark of strange alarms,
you will bear a child
lovelier than the wind's arms.'
'I dream you will sit upon
a chair of white carnation.
In my breasts I feel
the warm milk's vibrations.'
'God bless you, girl,
in moonlight badly clad,
your child will have on his breast
a birthmark and three scars.
God bless you, girl,
mother of a hundred dynasties,
a landscape of bandits
shines in your barren eyes.'

The child sang in the womb
of the startled girl's eyes.
Three bullets of green almond
trembled in his voice.

THE ARREST OF ANTONIO EL CAMBORIO
ON THE ROAD TO SEVILLE

Antonio Torres Heredia,
one of the Camborios,
with a walking-stick of willow
to the bullfight goes.
Dark from green moon,
casually, he strides,
and shining locks of hair
glint above his eyes.
Picking round lemons
halfway along the road,
he threw them into water
and it turned into gold.
Halfway along the road
under a huge elm
the Civil Guard captured him
and held him firm.

Evening draping its shoulders
slowly envelops the day,
over oceans and rivulets
it flourishes its cape.
The olive trees await
the Capricorn night until
a small breeze on horseback
leaps the leaden hills.
Antonio Torres Heredia,
one of the Camborios,
without his cane of willow
between the black hats goes.
Antonio, no true gypsy —
blood in jets should spurt!
You are no Camborio —

old knives shiver in the dust.
At nine that night
he was taken to the jail
while all the Civil Guards
sat drinking lemonade.
At nine that night
he heard the shooting bolt
while all the shining sky
glistened like a colt.

THE DEATH OF ANTONIO EL CAMBORIO

Voices of death
along the river breaking.
Ancient voices that enfold
a voice of male carnation.
Their thighs pierced by him
as if pierced by wild boars' teeth,
he leapt in the fight
as a smooth dolphin leaps.
He washed in enemies' blood
his crimson tie
but there were four daggers
and he *had* to die.
When the stars threw their spears
into the grey river
where the young bulls dream
veronicas of wallflowers,
voices of death screamed
along the Guadalquivir.

'Antonio Torres Heredia,
true Camborio relation,
dark from green moon,
voice of male carnation,
who took your life away
down by the Guadalquivir?'
'My four cousins took it,
the four from Benemji.
They did not envy in others
what they envied in me,
raisin-coloured shoes,
lockets of ivory,
and this skin with olive oil
and jasmine kneaded clean —

Federico García Lorca,
send the Civil Guards his way.
Already my waist has snapped
like a stalk of maize.'

He spurted three jets of blood
and lying in profile died,
his face an unrepeatable,
living coin.

DEAD FROM LOVE

What is that thing that shines
in the high corridors?
Eleven has just struck;
my son — shut the door.
In my unwilling eyes
four lanterns glare;
someone must be busy
polishing the copper.
Garlic of dying silver,
the waning moon lowers
yellow locks of hair
on yellow towers.
Night calls trembling
from the crystal chambers
pursued by a thousand dogs
she does not know;
a smell of wine and amber
comes from the corridors.

Breezes from soaked cane,
whispers of ancient voices
resound on the broken arches
of the deep night-time.
Roses and oxen sleep.
Alone in the corridors
the four lights shout
with the fury of St George.
Sad women of the valley
keep male blood quiet:
silence of cut flowers,
bitterness of young thighs.

Old women of the river
lament at the mountain's base
for some lost moment
of names and long hair.
Facades of whitewash make
the night bright and square.
Angels and gypsies gather.
Accordions play.

When I am dead
and buried with the lords
blue telegrams will go
from South to North.
Seven double poppies,
seven bloods and seven moans
in the dim chambers
crack the opaque moons.
Somewhere there resounds
a sea of vows
full of cut hands
and coronets of flowers.
The sky slams shut
on the abrupt noise of forest floors
while the lights cry out
in the high corridors.

BALLAD OF THE ACCURSÈD

In my peaceless solitude,
my body's small eyes,
my horse's huge eyes
never close at night,
nor look to the other side
where a dream of thirteen ships
in a silence glides.
Instead, clear and sharp
like ever-watchful guards,
my eyes look to a north
of metals and broken shards
while my body, without veins,
consults frozen playing-cards.

The heavy oxen of the water
charge the young male forms
who bathe in the moons
of their undulating horns.
Upon the sleeping anvils
the hammers sang with force,
insomnia of horseman,
insomnia of horse.

Amargo was advised:
you may cut if you wish
the flowers on your patio
on June the twenty-fifth.

Paint a cross upon your door
and put your name below
because hemlocks and nettles
from your side will grow,
and needles of wet lime

will eat into your toes.
It will be at night, and dark
through the magnetic hills
where the oxen of the water
in the rushes drink their fill.
Ask for lights and bells.
Learn to cross your hands
and enjoy the cold winds
of metals and broken ground.
Within two months
you will lie in a shroud.

On the twenty-fifth of June
Amargo's eyes were open,
on the twenty-fifth of August
the irises were broken.
Men came down the street
to see the accursèd one
where transfixed against a wall
hung peace, alone.
With its Roman-sculptured lines,
its square corners dumb,
the impeccable winding-sheet
gave death its equilibrium.

BALLAD OF THE SPANISH CIVIL GUARD

Black, black are the horses.
And the horseshoes are black.
On the cloaks shine out
stains of ink and of wax.
Their skulls are made of lead
and they cannot weep;
with their patent-leather hearts
they ride along the street.
These hunchbacked things of night,
wherever they crawl, command
silences of black rubber
and fears of fine sand.
They go where they wish to go
and hide inside their heads
a fearful vague astronomy
of ghostly bullet-lead.

O city of the gypsies!
At your corners flags fly,
your melon moon is full,
your cherries are ripe.
O city of the gypsies!
Who can forget you now?
City of musk and sorrow
and cinnamon-coloured towers.

When that night came —
O night of deepest night! —
the gypsies in their forges
made arrows and suns in fire.
A mortally wounded horse
knocked at all the doorways
and cockerels made of glass

sang in Jerez de la Frontera.
The wind turned the corner
naked in surprise
on that night, that silver night,
that night of deepest night.

The half moon was dreaming
the ecstasy of the stork;
and banners and lanterns
raid the roofs' flat tops.
Female dancers without hips
in the mirrors wailed,
water and shadow, shadow and water
at Jerez de le Frontera.

O city of the gypsies!
Who could forget you, once there?
Keep her away from the sea
without combs to part her hair.
O city of the gypsies!
At your corners flags fly,
but quench your green lamps:
the Civil Guard is riding by.

They advance two by two
into the festive town.
Their cartridge-belts give off
a murmur of graveside flowers.
They advance two by two,
double nocturnal blurs;
they imagine the sky to be
a window full of spurs.

All the clocks stopped
and the cognac on the shelf

changed into November
to protect itself.
A flight of loud screams
came from the weathervanes
and sabres cut the breeze
which the hooves had brained.
Along the streets in shadow
fled the gypsy women, old
with their sleeping horses
and their jars full of gold.

Up the steep streets
went the sinister cloaks
and silver in their wake
scissor whirlpools broke.
And by the Bethlehem gate
the gypsies find the ground
a saint hacked with wounds
putting a girl in shrouds.
Stubborn fusillades
spattered the night with jars.
The Virgin healed the children
with the saliva of the stars.
But the Civil Guard advanced
sowing their numerous fires
while, tender and naked,
imagination expired.
Rosa de los Camborios
sits moaning at her gate
with her hacked-off breasts
before her on a plate.
And the other girls ran
pursued by their long hair
while roses of gunpowder
exploded in the air.

O city of the gypsies!
The Civil Guard moved
through a tunnel of silence
while flames encircled you.
O city of the gypsies!
Who could forget this land?
On my forehead you shall be found.
Concerto of moon and sand.

In Memoriam David Hayes, Latin Teacher

from the Latin of Horace (Quintus Horatius Flaccus), 65-8 BC,
based on Odes IV vii

The snow is gone and the greenness
    comes back to the fields and trees;
Earth changes again and the rivers
    run shallower to the seas.

Young girls and their companions
    may dance on the mountain slope
but the hours that rob the good from days
    warn us not to hope.

The warm wind makes cold days milder,
    doomed Summer tramples the Spring;
as Autumn drops its apples
    dead Winter rushes in.

The changing moon renews the sky
    but when we go down, as we must,
to join the good and the rich and the wise,
    we become shadow and dust.

Once you are dead and God, he makes
    his final judgement clear,
no pull, no talk, no kickback
    will bring you back to here.

Who knows if God ensures
    tomorrow comes after today?
All that you spend on yourself
    will not go to a greedy heir.

Loyola can't save from darkness
    Father Hopkins pure and mild;
nor can the Sphinx break off the chains
    from her belovèd Oscar Wilde.

Delver

A version of a poem by the Latvian poet Imants Ziedonis (born 1933)

The soul is an archaeological site
and whoever digs there treads
on very dangerous dust.
Not only has the brain entombed
the very phantoms that would drive it mad
in its last sealed chamber,
it is as well the haunt
of history and the myths of night,
of mysteries of blood and bread,
of staghorned images of lust,
of creatures multi-nippled, multi-wombed:
so beware, red lady, Christianity-clad,
you may discover and unwrap
the bandage from a shape,
unknowable, but always there,
ahide in endless winding-sheets,
and then before you it may glow
like logs about to flare.
It is, perhaps, a secret;
so you, all eager, want to know
and keep unwinding layers
from this brittle onion-thing
that suddenly is very real
and very small
and is diminishing.
You fear it's lost. You stop,
your fingers sticky with old veils and robes.
But perhaps your brain's probes
have let loose the very phantom
that would drive it mad.
So beware, red lady, Christianity-clad.

Celebration

from the Irish of Nuala Ní Dhomhnaill (born 1952)

Rise, small bird, to the top of the tree
and clasp the topmost branch with your feet,
sing out from your throat
your torrent of glorious notes
and then your melody re-enact:
remind me, earthbound, of some basic facts —
say if love leaves me I'll hardly lose my mind
and though grief is great so's the music of life.

Rise and tell to us poor creatures
by your bursting *joie de vivre* and sweetness
that the cows low sweetly in river fields
with grass and wild flag up to their ears
chewing the cud with contented sighs,
trust and patience in the solemn eyes
though the butcher awaits them and liver-fluke
hides in the cresses of every brook.

Tell how headscarved women pray the ritual
in Minard at John the Baptist's well.
Come from Dingle and Camp, they start to sweat
in their crimplene dresses in August heat.
The fat one starts the Rosary chanting,
decades rise and fall in a rustic mantra
like corncrake-call or hum of bees
while fruitflies dust with eggs the blackberries.

Tell how a dolphin-like English girl
in a yellow bikini rides the sea-swell,
strides to the door of her caravan,
dries herself, striped towel in hand.
Tell how her belly is sun-browned,
her breasts like grapefruit full and round,

a hairbrush in her hand, a tube of *Loxene* gel —
a Venus without her scallop-shell.

Rise and sing though unaware
that a middle-aged woman is on her way,
depressed in the sand dunes, pushing for miles
a pram which contains a retarded child.
Her face is a picture of defeat,
her elastic stockings killing in the heat
but even worse, she'd know greater pain
without them from her varicose veins.

Sing out loud from the shade of your oak,
mistle thrush with your speckled throat
dazzling my eyes, sing while you can
to the still child in the small pram.
He will clap his hands and start to laugh
conveying this delight to his Mam:
'From your brooding take some ease,
hear the small bird on the top of the trees!'

The woman breaks through the fog around her,
her courage and sense again have found her.
In the flash of an eye a sun ray will fall
and she will smile through her self-pitying pall.
I prefer that smile to her depressed face —
you, small bird, deserve all praise,
your song is a witness to the pain and joy
that goes in hand with just being alive.

This Lonely Load

from the Irish of Nuala Ní Dhomhnaill

Take from me this lonely load —
don't stay and stare
behind the window-pane.
I cry
into my Guinness glass,
see me, see me
and embrace me.

Take from me this lonely load —
don't you hide
inside a fog of words.
We're lost in the same mist
on the cliff above the lake,
take my hand
and lead me from the abyss.

Take from me this lonely load —
the straddle of anguish
weighs me down daily,
unharness me
and perhaps I will be loyal
a little while
to him who minds me.

Take from me this lonely load —
around my body
tighten your snug arms.
Look into my eyes,
look well.
I will not be there
when we're mouth to mouth.

Oriental Morning

from the Irish of Nuala Ní Dhomhnaill

It's the early rising I hate most
and also fear the most —
a time when the world's deep asleep
(as it goes in the old poems);
no rover abroad, no wind in the trees,
a crimson sky, cut-nail moon
and one small star — easy to see
how the young sultan Mehmet II
saw the same in a bloody hoofprint
once on a battlefield and said,
'This is the only flag for my people
from now on.' It still is.

Strange metaphor. Telephone poles
threaten me. Foretelling danger electric pylons stride
bold on the plateau of Anatolia,
seven-headed monsters, seven-horned and -tailed
rushing towards me in seven league boots
declaring war on this impertinence of mine —
to come and rear my child within their bounds.
Soon one, like ragwort, will uproot a tree
and use it like a switch on us.

And where is the shining knight
who'll come to aid me,
who'll smash the challenge-pole to bits?
The man who'd earn his reward in war and hardship
and who would have to have his way
or let all rascals know the reason why?
Mettlesome man of great scruples
demanding justice, but only for himself,
a man who never fell on his arse,
who will not flee till hummocks flee.

It had to be that coming to this world
I was too greedy: that I chose
the big loaf and my mother's curse,
not the small loaf and her love;
that I refused the crumbs and burnt crust
of black bread to the skittering bird
that I met battered at the well;
that I refused the paw-hurt hound,
its pups outside for months: and thus
I would not help the hurt beasts
of the unconscious who begged of me
and whose gratitude would have set me free.

And so at dawn on this plateau
I have no neighbour's robin to sing bold
on a furze bush beside me
and inject some hope
or to remind me I am away too long
from my funereal women,
from those who'd place a wisp of straw
across my eyes to keep the crows away
from thoughts of how sheep are killed at home,
alas no small bird or bush I know.
I am totally wretched: deprived
of even the common archetypes.

Portrait

from the author's own Irish

I understand now the number that go
to the graveyard every day.
I understand the meaning of tears and kisses:
no one died when I was young.

On the table I put a mirror.
I take paper and pen in my hand.
In the fields children are increasing;
inside, my soul is getting smaller.

A frost-fall is in my hair,
burst blood-vessels in my face,
there is a staff on my forehead,
cacophonous music written by age.

I see now that I am one
of the pigs that are intently running
to the cliff-edge, furiously;
I am one of the leading pigs.

I understand now the number that go
to the graveyard every day.
I understand the meaning of tears and kisses:
no one died when I was young.

An Afterword

A note accompanying Michael Hartnett's *Tao* begins 'This is not a translation. I know no Chinese.' Frequently, in the course of his almost amphibious movement between languages which he *did* know, he took original poems and made new ones of his own. Nor could he say with certainty whether he wrote 'The Retreat of Ita Cagney' before 'Cúlú Íde' or *vice versa*. Which was the translation of the other? I believe he first wrote some lines in English, some in Irish.

Translation, he noted once, was a way of studying techniques, and in the course of four decades he made personal adaptations of poems to which he was attracted, often for their spiritual dimensions. His empathies became obsessions, particularly in his identification with the cultural turbulence of the lives of three seventeenth-century Irish poets.

The aim of this collection is to complement the books which were among Michael's final aspirations — *Collected Poems* (2001) and *A Book of Strays* (2002) — and his five volumes of translations, all of which remain in print: *O Bruadair* (1985), *Haicéad* (1993) and *O Rathaille* (1998); *A Necklace of Wrens* (1987), his own poems in Irish and English; and *Selected Poems* of Nuala Ní Dhomhnaill, published first by Raven Arts Press in 1986.

The assembly of these five books, along with the contents of *Translations*, would make an unwieldy single volume. So, this gathers fugitive and new pieces — the aforementioned *Tao*, poems from Old, Middle and Modern Irish (including a variant Ó Bruadair), his Lorca etc. The translations of Catullus and Heine, in which he was immersed in his final years, appear here for the first time. (I have preserved his arrangement of the Latin poems: the Roman numerals refer to standard editions.)

At no time in our discussions when we were preparing *Selected and New Poems* (1994) and the posthumous *Collected* did Michael propose including either poems in Irish or translations. I believe he lost faith in his own Irish following his 'return' to English. He never managed to complete the book (announced as *Daoine*) which he hoped would follow his first Irish collection, *Adharca Broic* (1978). Though he did publish in

Irish occasionally in the early 1980s 'Portrait' (page 124) is a version of one of the few poems which remain uncollected. Likewise, a book-length poem, *Stair na hÉireann*, came to nothing.

His interest in translation, however, never wavered. He had started work on Ramón Lull's *El Desconort*, the thirteenth-century Catalan song of desolation, ('God, with your grace, I commence this despair / which I sing to rid myself of care . . . ') and spoke of turning his hand to *Agallamh na Seanórach*. He planned more Catullus and Heine. What we have is a bonus.

I appreciate the support and assistance of Michael's partner, Angela Liston, and of his children, Lara (Goulding) and Niall. I acknowledge also the generous expertise of Máirín Ní Dhonnchadha and Durong Pu.

The book's title is the one Michael wanted.

Peter Fallon